Five A.M. in Beijing

FIVE A.M. IN BEIJING

Poems of China

Willis Barnstone

The Sheep Meadow Press
Riverdale-on-Hudson, New York

Acknowledgments

Some of these poems have appeared in the *Literary Review, Massachusetts Review, New Letters,* and *Prairie Schooner.* "Spirit Has a Beginning" received the Emily Dickinson Award in 1986 from the Poetry Society of America.

Printed in the United States of America

The Sheep Meadow Press, Riverdale-on-Hudson, N.Y.

Typesetting by Keystrokes, Lenox, Massachusetts

Distributed by Persea Books
225 Lafayette Street
New York, N.Y. 10012

Library of Congress Catalog Card Number: 86-43209

ISBN 0-935296-66-2
ISBN 0-935296-67-0 (pbk.)

In the ancient forest there is no human path.
A bell in the deep mountain. Where is it from?

Wang Wei (701–761)

Contents

for Lu Jie

I China Moon

Going Back to China

Outside, the full moon is memory light
knifing those of us who look up and remember.
People drive from blue house to blue house,
and I go back out there with them,
out of my own icestorm I'm sick of. Enough.
In a few weeks I'll return to China,
to Tu Fu wandering from exile to exile,
from childhood with a horse at dawn
to now with a few white hairs on his head,
still alive by scribbling out his poems,
his talking paintings.
I feel peaceful already.
I've not tried to conceal the weak eyes
of indecision
and soon will camp out in new drab rooms
in an empire city of red dust and rice,
alleys looming with white shirts and urine,
a shabby mansion jammed with Ming tables
where Wang Shixiang, back from work camps,
brushpens his unique scholarly books.
Already I wander frontiers of sleeping houses
on my one-gear bike; I smell mounds
of cabbage outside dank cement entryways;
am back to a half moon in Beijing,
to odd books with difficult characters
and a man unwillingly older
whom I wear without disdain and lightly.

Five A.M. *in Beijing*

Awake in darkness. A dream of thighs rips me
    out of sleep.
Outside the window in the carbon gas gloom
I hear the morning song of a gargling spitter
in the brick alley, tuning up like a baritone.
The city is wrestling with its throat
and searches deeper in its lungs for yellow pearls.
Near daybreak another spitter
warbles before casting his puddle in our ears.
Then air comes alive with screaky sparrows,
and someone is whistling
like the myna bird moon which flew so slowly out
of the night.

The stroller whistles a melody in the alley
as once from a predawn bed on Skyros
I heard my drunk Greek friends chanting all the way
across the pine winter island.
Another sick terrible cough. The whistling persists,
military and ancient. On the orange Xinjiang rug
I'm lying on my back,
hearing the call outside, ridiculous but hot and waiting
for song and ascension
as first rays ignite with December's foul smoke,
as breakfast hunger jostles my loose pajamas,
as time, which is our dream, the mechanical spy
    into the spirit,
pushes into gray factories growing in the dusk
and performs its second waking.

*Alone in China with Tu Fu Who Invites Me
to His Cottage to Drink 20 Cups of Wine
or to Climb into Clouds That Purge My Feelings*

Tu Fu, I keep meeting you on Boiled Rice Mountain
when the rest of the hemisphere is asleep
or making love or working in an all-night corrugated metal
        factory.
You fled officials under their umbrellas
and enjoy your sorrowful exile.
You watch the candle waste away in your room,
waiting for the gold lock to turn,
for the moon to hit the rafters of your cottage.

I look at your words and see we are both thinking
        very loud.
You tell me it would be wrong
not to see the blue boredom in a worker's eyes
along the ox-manured bicycle road
and just as wrong
not to watch him laugh suddenly wide as a white
        laundry bag
as he hams it up with a dripping shovel.
I close your book and bitch about the airless soul
        between poems,
go in circles about failure to love
or even to whisper correctly to a mountain or heron.
Can you tell me why feelings are so tepid
unless we slip into a pit of disasters?

Tu Fu, you drink and write alone for twelve hundred years,
a continent in your brushpen,
and things I bellyache about of course you complain of
        and poignantly,
as we converse alone, and I am always happy
with your swans white as the sun
surprising spring onions in the evening rain

while millions of peasants strangely sleep outside
     your song
and don't drink hot water like us.

You scratch the scant hair on your white head,
look for a hairpin, utterly sad,
stealing life for your old age. Yet rain
falls into your courtyard as through childhood.
It falls on your daughter whom you sing
into twilight. With all your talk
I notice on the Mountain of Boiled Rice
you still wear your bamboo hat at noon.

Walking the City of Poplars

The poplars are ancient signs of forests
amid the Beijing smell of coal and noodles.
Wherever I go, at the outdoor market
where a lady with leather between her teeth
whirls on a cobbler's dirty stool
and hammers nails into my sole and heel,
in line for apples at a table leaning full
like a jalopy in a puddle,
or by the doorway of the department store
where I get a fuse,
wherever I go the poplars in autumn wind glitter.

Even in the Great Hall of the People
where we stand up again and again to toast the vice-
    prime minister
and local bosses and each other,
where columns and carpets are clean
as Tsarist Moscow's great cream-colored dining rooms,
I remember light emerging from poplar leaves
in the jammed street by Purple Bamboo Park
or see aspens shiver transparent outside my window
as they always shivered, even in Han or Paleozoic sun.

As I leaf through a museum book, not wanting to think,
I luckily find an old silent painting
where poplars neither ask nor hear transcendental words.
In this Buddhist scene the mountain and cloud,
the forest with calligraphic branches,
are no more nor less than a figure on the rim of
    oncoming night.
One tree is falling—time also stands in the air—
into the glitter of poplars where a hermit is fussing
around a cottage on his hill.

Cycling Home on My Flying Pigeon

For hours I've been pumping my Flying Pigeon
behind fire of ancient bus fumes
and swarms of slow peddlers playing chicken with trucks
past the village idiot
whose fat tongue rises to his crooked eyes
as he twists his head to survey the jammed commercial
    backstreet.
My pack hurts me, my own tongue is sore
and the new moon sings over the zoo and huge gray
    buildings
on the longest streets in the world.

My bike clanks in the dusk, rattling like sudden summer
    hail
in the corridors of the Summer Palace.
Before a building of gates and towering letters
the street is pulsing with white-shirted couples
    dancing a tango,
not a Chinese but the old Argentine *"A media luz."*
The booming song endures for blocks.
A bus almost hits me. I'm careless now.
In half light I cross the last August day
with my heart in arctic heat.
Who is alone when death lingers in my old house
    across the ocean
or a child stares doll-eyed out of the wooden-box sidecar?
Someone, riding up beside me, smiles HELLO.

Snow

Although Wang Wei is peaceful looking at
the apricot, the sea gull and the frost
climbing the village hills, or feels the mat
of pine trees on the mountain sky, or lost
in meditation loses nature and
the outer light and sings his way through mist
inside, although Wang Wei becomes the land
and loitering rain, his mountain clouds exist
in poems—not in life—and turn like mills
never exhausting time. Wang Wei also
was stuck in life, and from his hermitage
he tells a friend to walk the idle hills
alone, to swallow failure like the age-
ing year, to dream (what else is there?) of snow.

Walter Whitman

In fairly good health, fifty-six years old, a child
     of oriental adventure,
I ask you to look for me.
I am the stranger I cannot find.
If you want me, read me under these words.
They prove my grounds for extreme pessimism:
their banality, low soul, their rambling effort to sing
     myself
in their alphabet utterly deprived of grace.

But I don't accept my death. The notion sickens me,
especially in half sleep
when blank, in terror, I wake as a fetal ball.
I don't accept my age and work to cover it
with each shampoo, striped shirt, each dawn jog
outside the gates around the Youyi Binguan,
and brood, less than before, about an insipid life.

I wait for everything, good poems, for you to think so,
a woman I'll want, who will want me.
Surprisingly, though my candle is lower each day,
I'm confident, I suppose.
Empty now, with love lost many times, a fussy man,
I'm lucky to want,
to sit in an easy chair in the City of Red Dust
in the Friendship Hotel,
to return from my impassioned lecture on heroic Walt
and know myself Walter with some rooms in Brooklyn,
to assume the world, the mud under my bicycle.

Roof Party at the Institute

On an antique fish I floated down to megalopolis
with its dusty rugs and temple columns of red blood
and guards walking in green laundry bags with stars
    looking from their hats,
and other men at gates in ordinary clothes
who watch.

I love my friends. We conspire.
They tell me of the Great Wall around their unit,
of green guards at the doors.
The old scholar takes me by the wall on the roof
and tells me in careful Oxford speech,
"I hung my head low and to the side when they beat me,
supposing even then they were right,
that Mao *had* to be right."
He sips a beer. Someone comes and we stop,
now strangers.

The old scholar goes home for the night.
I am like the country, understanding little,
always beginning.
How have I reached an age where I sleep alone?
Such solitude, isn't it barbaric?
The lousy loudspeaker pumping out minority dances
is deserted.

The night is a dark and mystifying hill,
the mind and these longest streets unknown
like 5,000 Chinese characters.
I kick up the stand, slip in the key, and board
    my cranky bike.
A cockroach circling a glass tabletop,
I pedal awkwardly through a green wind.

A few men squat vacantly on the curb.
At my hotel the guards gaze through me.
Under low constellations and fires icing the evening air
the night smells of jasmine and urine.

All in Daily Misery

Outside your room the latrine sings its flower
of strangeness. Inside, the fluorescent bulb
dreams blue on your poster and the cement floor,
on the guitar you carefully play
as afternoon performs a few acrobatic leaps
        with its gold egg
and darkens our quick walk into winter and to supper.

Thank you for letting me share the tasty lotus
and bamboo. I suppose as an earlier ghost
I worked as a butler in the cruel empress's palace
or stole and poached
whereupon they shaved my head and helicoptered me
into a remote minority desert
where I began my life sentence on roads that don't
        go out,
and while my compassion overflows for us and all
in daily misery, I ask for honey
to liven my dessert. Thank you again.
Don't let me forget the victims in manure fields
        and tea farms,
the criminals with boards around their necks,
loaded on the truck for the single shot in the head,
and us in the dining room where I feel you so close
I squeeze my cloth napkin by the huge calligraphy
        on the wall
so as not to break.

Oilcloth Covered Tables with Potted Flowers

After supper I am talked out. The moon is yellow
and has forests of stone hands
that keep it from singing.
After drinking sweet wine and digging into Mongolian
    hot pot,
after euphoria and shaking hands with the cook,
I'm outside the red building with Wang
    who reminds the moon
of her old drinking companions, Li Po and his shadow,
who jumped up to a river of stars.
I'm all talked out. The rusty gate drifts
around the compound like a fisherman lying in his boat,
wandering in a peaceful garden lake
others call the soul. The moon's hands are green.
I've one less day in my life.
The old school's locked up, the city closed.
It's only eight
but a Buddhist flute works up to heaven.
Soon I'll be back in my chair, trying to turn
    into books.

Hanging Around Beijing

Circling and circling through alleys,
by watch shops where young women like nurses operate
    intently with tiny screwdrivers
to fix hairsprings of time,
by a small cheap rug store
and a steamy Muslim mutton eating place,
I get to a flower garden wall facing a vast exploding
    intersection.
Trucks blunder through with men and boys sleeping spread-eagle
    like corpses
on cabbages in the beds.

Oblivious to pollution, to winter roses
just behind the wall,
to women round like white nuns in gauze hats, sweeping
    the gutters,
I stay at least 10 years fixed and lost
in my shabby outfit and mismatching stockings.
I'm killing the day with no one,
perfectly deep and ignorant amid new shabby concrete
    structures
and policewomen lightly holding hands as they patrol.
Dirt blows in my eyes. Smell of mules blows through
the jammed streets like a ballad.

The sand in my eyes causes a black crescent moon
to float placidly around my head.

Some old gentlemen standing around with birdcages wait
like me, and say nothing
though they peer at people and up at blue lakes mapping
    the sky
with its islands of immortality.

While occupied in not dreaming up ultimate females
        for later lives,
in not inventing truth,
I kill a day-off in Beijing
with the old gentlemen companions through the morning.

Their cages are ancient
with myna birds from before the dynasties of *homo
        erectus.*
Giving the birds air, they pick the cages up sometimes.
In oblivion I stick to my rocky seat on a wall.

Brooding on Wangfujing Street

After love we talked, loved again and slept till fall
        morning sunny over plants
was sea gulls in our closed eyes. Shall we hug
four more days? Through afternoon we read half naked
on the rug, unable to find our Sunday clothes.
I don't look for you
tonight as I walk back Wangfujing Street.

Four years have left my mind. Yet till the last
ride home from the furniture stripping shop
and our kiss—no kiss is final—when our faces mingled,
I denied the planet could split forever into ghosts
        and memory.
I can't look for you: not for passion
and hurt and the intense soul of our silly rampage
        through tulip tree ravines,
nor for our laughter of crazies
or pacing at a corner without warm clothes a savage
        December night,
or waiting while I had crawled inside a phone
for your maybe coming in the morning.

No more. I won't look in the Foreign Expert Dining Hall
        for you choosing vegetables for us,
I won't expect us to walk near the perfumed palace
        of the late emperors in Chengde.
You see I never construe you, you're never alive
        like the cock
fulminating through dawn,
we're never together four days on northwest trains
where tribesmen pull turnips from violet fields.

I've proved that even China, truth, and our beds
floating on two radically colored oceans
can't shake you out of me.
In cool exotic Whitewater, Wisconsin, someplace
off a Sunday road, you go with your shadow hiking
        through a forest burning red.
The stores on Wangfujing are shut. I drift
into a silk and charcoal alley, hop over a trashcan.
My body, empty of spirit, persists in learning
nothing at all.

If You Climb the Stone Stairs

If you climb the stone stairs and knock at the door
    at three in the morning,
we'll go down to Shandong,
the coast where Confucius collected virtue;
dusk will glide against us at the hour
climbers make base camp, spend the night plotting
snowtrails before the plunge
up to the top of the world.
We'll wake to hunger, aware on my birthday
of being trapped, as Manichaeans warn, in bodies
which are our mystery.

A year ago I was waiting for the knock,
and you laughed in and looked at me with love,
    I guessed.
We got undressed to shower. You held me
in your two hands while we kissed.
You had a gift or two—I can't remember what
    they were—O yes, shaving soap
and an Italian mug.
Even my apartment that I hated, its warm wood floors
    and Pakistan rugs,
the antique puncheon pine blanket chest, the Olmec wrestler,
looked good.

These pictures keep me from sleeping. I get up,
fumble to the hot water thermos.
A few stars outside the window promise more hours
    of mania.
I see through a great hole to the other globe
where you are using a jeweler's tools
to play with words.

Even now when time is left over and hope imposter
I feel you at my smoky table, seldom near enough.
I'm in two bodies at once. Acacia tree, revelation.
It's a year. Can you come to Beijing for just
        a few hours? We'll be lost
down in Shandong for good. Dusk will glide through us
and light our bodies inside.
When you show up, we'll walk with Confucius
sloshing in rice paddies,
with snow and mountain time in our pockets,
        when you come.

Seeing Zu Off at Qizhou

Only just now we met and laughed
yet here I'm crying to see you off.
In the prayer tent we are broken.
The dead city intensifies our grief.
Coldly the remote mountains are clean.
Dusk comes. The long river races by.
You undo the rope, are already gone.
I stand for a long time, looking.

Wang Wei (701–761)
translated by Tony Barnstone,
Willis Barnstone, and Xu Haixin

Cristoforo Colombo

1

Night is greenly cold and your face appears
down an ignorant alley.
I'm circling my walled hotel in running shoes.
I don't invent the night.
In the mornings I know blood will surface if my razor
     daydreams
or my eyes will ache pleasantly in working out Wang Wei's
characters that tell how
three white birds come after white rain to his empty
     mountain.
So why not let the mind drift?

2

Cristoforo Colombo was no madman to dream up a round globe
     of spices and oceans.
He wrote cordial letters to the Catholic queen
so he could sail,
and the court astrologer Sima Qian, castrated by Wu Di
for audacity of words,
was no charlatan for writing that Emperor Shi Huangdi
lay in a tomb with 10,000 clay soldiers.
He was no crazier
than Schliemann digging level after level for Troy
or Colombo wanting a new Silk Route and spice.

3

I am eager as the animals Colombo took on the Niña,
gazing out merely at water.
Why not reach a sanctuary of birch forests and beasts
     unmapped by sailors?

Aching a bit from the hardening road, I run all eyes,
swerving to miss cars, eating a cake of fire,
inspecting the moon that forgot to die,
inspecting green nights through the black window
     of the heart.
Then weary with illusion, weary, a bit weak,
I defend the ministry of reason,
but not for long.
It is 1492 again, year of the Niña,
and everywhere I see Colombo gazing out at water.

The Pungent Smell of China

1

Each afternoon I pedal home from work
like a ghostly robot amid slow cycling gangs
in dreary Mao caps.
The imperial city is shorn of its city wall.
Women ride with coarse nets draped on their faces
against sandstorms in the huge squares,
I try to skirt around lumps of muleshit.
Through a break in the street wall
I make out Fragrant Mountains in the west
sleeping in their violet elephant wrinkles.
The slopes have a wildflower tang,
Sunday fresh. I guess their smell
as Gobi winds float dust into the city's soft coal haze.

2

Beijing is demolishing its smoky wooden rooms.
Cranes with giant beaks and legs migrate out of
    the marshes
and stride into construction sites,
balling down wretched smelly huts, their door carvings
and crooked iron windows.
They step through mud brick alleys and a rare mansion
with orange roofs
yet somehow spare noisy Great Street of the Gate
    Facing the Sun
or herb shops and theaters on Great Barrier Lane
with its old rambling bordello now a silk store.

3

As when a mob of Christian monks clamored outside the house
of the beautiful Hypatia of Alexandria,
and stoned her to death,

liberating the city from its last pagan philosopher,
so Beijing bids goodbye to the open sewers,
to the jasmine courtyards and forest of old streets
it is losing,
to scented rooms, to a shadow of a body
haunting like opium and sin,
to a Taoist sanctuary filled with superstition
    and books,
and the pungent smell of China that is leaving.

Gospel of the Mountains

On a red mountain north of Beijing (where
the Chinese hermits banished morning frost
by chopping wood) the wisdom of the air
washes the silent herons. Time is lost
like a smoke wisp hanging over bamboo.
Time of no mind. The mountain cherries bloom
by the white hut, and life is never through
although the heart can never leave its room.
One life, caught on the planet, never with
the burning spice of immortality.
On a red mountain, mist and sunlight hold
some peaceful lemon trees in their own myth
of wisdom. God's disease of history
is out of place, and lemon air is cold.

Adventure of the Heart

Shanghai. I smell my fear among the smells
of medicine and patients in the hall.
The nurse ties on my mask, quietly impels
me toward the table, but I hug the wall.
Hard to witness the bloody cut mushroom
of a man's heart. His eyes are open as
he sips a bit of juice, and the perfume
of death drips off a nylon thread which has
repaired the shadow of a soul. His ear
holds one electric needle, quivering.
The eyes call out. I think about crazed Lear
carrying his daughter, drownings off Vietnam,
my coffined mother on the train. All being
trembles for breath. All praise of dark is sham.

Words on Rice Paper

I'm back in exile but my words are mine,
down in the unwalled trunk of papers
in my heart. I ship them with me to all ports,
even here where people speak in four tones.
They are my secret force and I'm safely unknown
as I walk by a lady street sweeper
with a white gauze hat low on her face.

It's better this way. If someone knew,
I wouldn't scrabble through the night
scratching words up from my unwilling underworld
        posing as darkness,
or be fanatic like the nocturnal possum
outside our Indiana barn,
rattling around in a metal garbage bin, stealing
        food.
I'm free to scrawl miles of poems on rice paper
since I'm alone and keep losing love.

But if I had love and walked with her many days
in that strange forest of wrestling rhododendra,
if I were happy and made out maroon dresses
through the incense of the Chengde temple and its single
        Lama monk,
if I came home
and the secret mountain where I sleep and live,
its inner hill of words,
were flagrantly turned into public books,
I'd be cheerfully ridiculous, leap up clicking heels,
jump from sofa to chair to sofa;
my heart would expand perilously complete
and in all that light it would break apart,
full of rushing illumination.

Meeting Near the Summer Palace

1

Sima Qian, ancient historian of China, wrote precise
    tales like Han fables.
Like Sima I want to be truthful about us:
I could love you.
The symptoms of affliction were clear when you rose
    from the bed,
helping a fool write out a Buddhist character.
I was sitting behind, watching you.
Later in the taxi, a new Datsun, you said you'd call
and I shouldn't forget your name.
When you come we'll meet outside my compound,
maybe the Russian restaurant out by *Yiheyuan,*
    the Summer Palace,
small and white like a Greek *taverna* except for chopsticks,
butterfly menus and borscht.

2

Sima Qian spent his life telling stories
that the emperor didn't like. He trusted the page
as you trust me.
Conspiring, open and Tong-gang silent,
we work against fear under the castle of the power
    state,
against the tongue of neighborhood spies.
Even your Chinese name I mustn't record or give clues
about your profession.

On afternoons I sail by the guards without getting off
my bike as commanded by the sign for *waiguoren,*
    foreigners:
DISMOUNT FROM BICYCLE AT GATE
The guards shout *Xia che!* Down from vehicle!,
they grab for my sleeve, but I am gone.

I'm angry you can't break rules with me. You like me,
we talk in your dreams, you say,
and your rage is deeper by dynasties than mine.
One night we take bus 332, squashed into intimacy,
and secretly find our place. In our night,
freezing at a small table amid worker patrons
playing checkers, smoking, indifferent to us
in the fuming room,
we order dark wine, act free and drink borscht.
You are a tall moon, candid, lovely,
but let another Sima Qian record the truth.

At the Moscow Restaurant by the Zoo

We meet outside the gate to avoid signing in.
"I am Chinese," you say. I'm more comfortable
tonight than any night in China.

We eat at the Moscow Restaurant near the zoo,
in the foreign part, Old World and quiet,
where you can't go alone.

The stroganoff is cold but good. We don't drink
alcohol. They close early and we're out
by the big-character posters

in Beijing's first winter freeze. No taxi
so we walk to a nearby hotel you can't
enter without me.

"This is China," you remind me. We talk
for three hours. I'm happy, sip hot water
and eat pinguo pie.

Your eyes couldn't keep staring at me
with laughter, with doubt and elegance,
if you'd not been "sent

down to the countryside." We're back
outside on enormous streets. I don't
feel guilty for being

a foreigner. I'm not. We walk in Beijing's
first winter freeze. I know the crowds,
I'm at home. I don't

want to leave one day. "We'll meet when
I'm back from Manila." You're translating
Kafka's letters

to his sisters. "Don't talk about my plans
or I'll lose my job." After nine o'clock
in the city there is

no place but people. It's a rich night,
better than one day when we're not
in danger. We find a cab.

The driver likes us and charges half fare.
We're a slaphappy people, all of us roaming
through faith. Back at the gate

you keep the cab. I'm about to bang on the window
to say a last word. The cab pulls off. I know
you'll call in the early morning.

Reading Li Qingzhao

Reading the lonely poems of Li Qingzhao,
seeing her lying drunk, her hairpins on
the courtyard table as she mourns the bamboo
bed empty of her legal lover, gone
beyond the sky and her apricot tree,
I know those geese and bugles that explode
her evening in the late Song dynasty
signal her unique sorrow on the road
of the blue lotus. There by the Eastern Wall
her lord and friend fell into mist. Yet in
that same small garden of the scholar's house
they shared a passion for old scrolls, and when
he went (turning her moon to ink), in all
the world her grieving happened only once.

Coal Dust

As winter begins to chill and darken
and people get out their gauze masks,

coal furnaces kick on and pollution
inks the horizon. Smell is memory.

I'm in London, closing the window
in the boarding house toilet. Cold

filthy air has killed eleven bulls
on exhibit, and one foggy dawn

a car hits a horse-drawn milk wagon
and milk lakes the road, or some years

earlier in Paris I'm carrying books
back from the Sorbonne. The medical

students are singing dirty songs
and someone on a monument at the Odéon

says he'll piss on Charles de Gaulle
and the crowd shouts *pissez, donc!*

as he streams into the dusk. Air here
smells like Clapham Common, forgotten

till these mornings when the stairway
to my Beijing rooms has the same odor

and I'm back, young, beginning a decade
in Europe, a cafe revolutionary

carrying banners, A BAS LES FASCISTES,
sirens howl and *les flics* whirling clubs

charge into us. Dark coal fumes
of Chinese factory air put remembered

days into my blood where they circle
from heart to brain to heart,

and though Blake is dead his satanic mills
fill the sky with malignant aroma,

with memory before my birth, cheerful
eagerness of a young man learning

from the tree of Paris, or confusion
about a smoky future and its few hours,

now, drinking dumpling soup in an all-night
fuming cafe for Chinese workers

where Wang Jihui tells me all about orchards,
the market smell of a single persimmon

and price of coal. Outside, blue men on bicycles
bob through the smog like steel skeletons,

and one yellow apple, with seeds above
the killing smoke, lingers in the galaxies.

In a Beijing Monastery

Before the gold Buddha, the monk will be all
        night
in meditation posture. In the dark room
I thought he was the statue. When
the old teacher throws on the light he remains
        a circle.

*

By the marble stele, in the sun,
two shaved novices are playing badminton.

*

The old teacher demonstrates how to lie on our face
        before the reclining Buddha,
the huge one with slit eyes an inch from death.
We take turns—Jie, Guo, the malcontent driver—
to lie down, hands by our head, palms up.

*

I too am unattached. But if one is enlightened
that's another illusion.

Occasionally it is good to see the mind performing
its act, to stay back and watch
the lines of words wildly circling in place.

*

A novice in sagging trousers walks, reading sutras
        loud in the courtyard.

*

Time again. The sun leaves its meditation of light,
its meditation of the small darkening ball of earth
smelling of snow. It is snowing:

36

millions of white eyes are dropping down from
    night heaven
over White Cloud Temple,
over brick public latrines
where women with enormous blue coats squat in the dark,
over hospitals with bits of death and lanes of life,
over crowded rooms and late, almost empty, buses
rumbling through each unique second.

Millions of white eyes are dropping down on
guards smoking in alleys and experts in offices
full of illumination.

*

In the Buddha
perfect form meets perfect emptiness of life.
It is a wood image, surviving revolution,
holding a gold scepter and a bell.
The monk in his brown robe is a circle waiting
    for morning.
The Buddha is infinitely blind to snow.

Going to Temples outside Chengde

1

In the morning dining room it's wonderful alone
with sun and a few voices from the kitchen.
My table is nice with hot milk and jam.
In the corner friends are washing dishes.
Downtown air outside is dirty ancient mist
but in an hour I'll be walking by the last leafed trees
at the Tibetan temple on·the green slope:
the Temple of Universal Joy.
I'm in the happiest mood, eating, reading poems
    of George Seferis,
ready to float up to the giant Bodhisatva
with forty-two wooden arms
and forty-five eyes on its palms and face.

2

Outside the temple wall three farmers are haying
on their own earthen stage,
unaware they are being used for these lines.
If Corot were Chinese he would have liked
the morning shadows and light on their faces,
flickering yet poised in the still frame
    of distance.
Three farmers (one a woman) wave their sickles
like batons before an orchestra of wheat.
In country air of late autumn China,
some crows, black as factories and ignorant of sutras,
jar the sky, screeching. Below them,
impatient farmers laboring 2,000 years,
squinting faces from the underworld,
raise their sickles in these same fields of light.

A Day of a Life

Half past twelve. How the time has gone by.
Half past twelve. How the years have gone by.
These words are from Constantine Cavafy
who lit his lamp, sat without reading
for three hours, completely alone in his house,
remembering the shade of his younger body.

I come awake slowly, creased like an old boot,
but wet out quickly in the shower with curtains
sagging like eyebags. The *China Daily*'s already
under the door, with headlines of prosperity
or how many Vietnamese killed by guerrillas
in Campuchea, but I turn to the sports page

to baptize the fully useless news of tennis.
Now the thermos bottle gives me tea water
and I remember. Half past eight. Too late
for dining room. So I eat rolls at my desk
and think of all the people I want to call
across the oceans. They would restore me.

In the afternoon I ink thoughts into an envelope,
sending one letter to the sun, one to each
of you, changing character like Bolivian
heads of state and reproach my shallow mind.
An hour later I'm leaping up the steps
of the lovely sordid school, down the hall

smelling of chalk and piss, past Rumanian,
the Party Unit, the Dean of English, to my
own students, conspirators, in whom I lose
myself. OK, laugh at how I butcher your names!
We are all poets on Thursdays. I soar
because I'm with you now, nowhere else

unless we fly out the window in a gang
of seven pigeons cooing the way Tang pigeons
greeted our Buddhist poet when he went back
to his cottage deep in the wood. Half past eight
in my friendship rooms with Russian ceilings
arrogantly high, I flop in bed to moon

about the loneliness of life. The books
are on the floor, my eyes locked dark away
in a keyboard, and my body on a standard
blanket. Mind, heart, body. I can't do much
to change them. I'm not profound. I was born
this day. Half past twelve. How time has gone!

How do I lie completely alone in sheets,
not naked, wearing socks? I never recognized
the women when they gave themselves to me,
clean as Botticelli. Fool of guilt, I had to wait
for another clearer voice. Half past three.
High and awake, at last I feel my thoughts.

To My Cousin Qiu, Military Supply Official

When young I knew only the surface of things
and studied eagerly for fame and power.
I heard tales of marvelous years on horseback
and suffered from being no wiser than others.
Honestly, I didn't rely on empty words;
I tried several official posts.
But to be a clerk—always fearing punishment
for going against the times—is joyless.
In clear winter I see remote mountains
with dark green frozen in drifted snow.
Bright peaks beyond the eastern forest
tell me to abandon this world.
Cousin, like Huilian your taste is pure.
You once talked of living beyond mere dust.
I saw no rush to take your hand and go—
but how the years have thundered away!

Wang Wei (701–761)
translated by TB, WB, XH

China Moon

The air has cleared some with the cold. The moon
is growing toward December fullness. That dead
beauty keeps me warm and off-the-planet inside
as I bike against windy Siberia in the streets
to a cadre restaurant where I go to think
and eat. Fishbones on the floor. Words on the wall
I can't decipher. How can I be serious in a land
where I'm illiterate? So I joke a lot, nutty
as never before, with laughing friends in dreary

coats. I'm jammed in the free market where sweepers
push trash into our feet. The fishlady coughs
on my throat. The bicycle repairman is infinitely
tired smashing pedals into place. The moon
is grease in his eyes. In mine she's growing again
like time never turning back to recount a birth
of first dawn seen on Earth's first sabbath. Chinese
say God wasn't almighty since he had to rest
after just a few days work. In this Prussian

winter city I am in a garden of the crowds
where I merge glad, hoard each new word, in rooms
where the moon comes down to console a white page
with poems. When I'm downcast, missing you
whom I must deaden my heart to, the world
kicks at my door. I pay the laundry woman
who may be my aunt. I yawn uncontrollably
during the *hanyu* class though my teacher
with seven layers of clothing against December,

could be my mother. But the moon persists
in her blind profession, saying nothing
as I turn her blue dust into ink. Always,
when I'm finally alone, when I can't think
or feel the world, she is the companion

of the poem. Moon and paper marry. I take
the virgin sheet and fill it from the tree
of letters, and listen. I have no wife
but hear words, which come and are entombed,

hear the moon who talks until daybreak;
then go out to greet the night watchman and ask
where he put the shining mirror of time
as Persians called their heavenly body, and stroll
in empty Bamboo Park. When I face the sorrow
of ignorance on these nights, when ignorance
devours coming time and to live is to ache
in the airless chambers of ignorance, I face
the moon—with her silent trees—and eat her.

II   Bright Morning of Winter

Dreams and Memories on an Ordinary Evening in a Russian-built Apartment

So many dreams keep turning me back to life.
When out in the old frosty alleys,
which I always think must go somewhere,
when weariness cries inside,
weighing down to water under the city
where cockroaches live in huge sewers,
when I'm little more than a sentimental pot
      of longing,
when reasons for pity burn clouds under my heart,
so many dreams turn me out:

Vicente in Madrid and his poems recorded from unremembered
      dreams,
whose death came wickedly to him this week,
or my father who tries to come back in dream enacted
      only in China,
or Miriam outside Jerusalem, with her spices
for the real body next to the open cave,
or Lu Jie in her Norwegian sweater
squashed together with me on the bus near the zoo,
soon to walk two blocks to the public bath.

So many dreams keep turning me back to life.
When you, Lu Jie, leave (you are being wheeled away
illegally on the back of a bike)
I remember Li Po's horse whinnying impatient
      at departure,
but in a year I know our midnight will return.
As I pass the bakery I take the moon,
wrap it in raw silk and place it in my suitcase
where it waits perfectly ready
for our next all-night walk on freezing roads.

Thinking of the Underground Poet Bei Dao and of Myself, Whom No One Will Put in Prison Because of What I Write

Even here in Asia I can think of nine ways
of being dishonest about poems I copy from nocturnal
    clouds
when I need to sleep.
Their unique reader, I play them like solitaire,
shuffling Queens and trying not to cheat.
At least I care for them.
But many are old cheap overcoats.
I feel sick.
Sometimes I smack into them like a typhoon
(to use a Cantonese word) and blow away half
    a wardrobe.
It's honey when bad poems are gone.

But how is it being their sole reader?
Do I make it as a stoic, winking at time, peacefully
    wise?
At all this I'm a flop.
Like centuries of the Wandering Jew
looking through continents into the anxious rooms
    of poets,
I spend my evenings with young Chinese friends
who are like me
waiting through the night in their chairs.

***With Bei Dao and His Painter Friend in a Place
Halfway down a Hutong in South Beijing***

Last night Bei Dao (who braved those years of writing
        for "Freedom Wall,"
who enjoyed wide readership by the Secret Police),
a young painter and I were shivering
in the artist's room in Beijing's coldest December
        of 20 years.
I warmed up by drinking hot water.
The poet and painter went out for wine so we could be
        Persian
and mix alcoholic dream with our smoke.
In this city of hidden artists
we all pontificated and were profound.
Listening to Bei Dao so many dynasties patient,
hearing a scratchy Beethoven sonata tape he put on
        for me,
I was honored and restored
by our elegant poverty, by books on the cold floor.

Bright Morning in Beijing

On our first night we sing all night in our sheets,
but as daybreak illumines orange cranes,
its needles of fire cross the city
and pierce our silky window. You worry,
ask me to leave first, walk down the stairway
and wait in the lobby of the Peace hotel.
But I can't find the door to the stairs,
openly take the lift, it doesn't matter,
and we walk out together,
down Gold Fish Alley to Wangfujing
where my favorite Uigurs sit on the street railing.
In their tough-guy 1930s caps and striped suits
they raise my spirits. We take a narrower street
toward breakfast at the Beijing Hotel,
and it begins to snow. First snow in Beijing.
Bicycles slow down. We feel like gods
dancing on the whitened street. We issue happiness
to the blue figures who walk around us
enjoying our joy.

China Songs

1

Chinese half moon, piece of jade,
a bowl of rice to feed the stars,
out in the West you were a gambler,
putting a new face on each night.
Here I take you back to my room
and sit you on my bamboo sheets.
You kiss me. So I wake from
being awake. One day they cut
off my hands and I wasn't even
a guitarist. You kiss me whole.

2

Why do I love you? I wrote you
a secret letter. And you sent
me cinnamon apple pie and words
I had no glasses to read. And soon
we were lovers. Yes, in China,
where love is ancient as lions
sleeping out in persimmon wind.
Will you ever leave me? I knock
on the door of the rain. We run
back into the mist to be alone.

3

Are you really bored? You gaze
at the fruitwagon like a gazelle
in Sinai baffled before a Hebrew
verse carved into the desert hill.
Don't worry. We're all just wise.
You took the train and I met you
on a sunny spring day. Isn't that
everyone's dream? Don't you know

one day we'll all descend into
yellow springs and live forever dead?

4

Don't be unhappy. Time is good.
So good each second we are breathing
bread. What's a little despair to
the orange tiles of a long dynasty?
China is more than a plate. My Greek
friend wrote that wherever he goes
the marble wounds him. How lucky
to be ancient! China is a world
of one woodcutter in the mountain,
O hermit, yes thunderously quiet.

5

You're good. This is the good night.
I'm jumping out of my sky because
you're so warm. Don't abandon me.
We slept alone for centuries.
I put on my shirt, took your hand
and found what sleep alone never
gave me. You. We were born alone
from night into gold. I've waited
all blood long. It's easy. I sing
and gamble, lost in our jade moon.

Ways of January 2, 1985

1

Since angels are soulless they cannot speak.
My heroes are the great failures of being,
Quevedo, Kafka and Cavafy, who saw night
at noon, tormenting the memory of sun,
who returned, lost, to their fatal aloneness.
I should sleep deep, be healthy, it's 2 again,
but I yield to waking to a solitude,
a way waiting for you to glance at this.

2

I try to know myself. Can a shadow study
a mirror? And my gazing inside is word
free. I feel it, and journey back to a warm
loud galaxy. The brain has noisy hands.
The mind is thunder! I understand nothing
and wonder if there is time. I suppose
there is only time, time the mouth eating
us bit by bit. I fear time's unheard end.

3

I don't want much. O yes, I wish you could
be here, reading this with me. Include me
in your solitude. You the anonymous
dust I never see (who's read none
of these poems), I confess I speak always
to you. But I care more for another
love who excels you. She has many names.
The weight of knowing is an ancient marble

4

statue Cavafy woke with in his arms, can't
put down, whose hands disappear and come back

mutilated. Yet I stumble into words
and besides have a few terrible secrets
sickly and better forgot. The screened window
is open to let twilight come. I forget
how I might have walked into a white vision,
into chance flight through a door of pain.

5

The Spaniard, Jew and Greek are my heroes.
Pain gave them lucidity, formula
of pathos. I am their anonymous dust
whose way is feeling. The Chinese tiger drawn
crudely and taped on my wall seems to know
whom he wants to terrify. Tonight I feel,
and round the globe are comrade fools. Be near.
Pain is a small star we all eat to live.

John Berryman in Beijing

1

After reading through the night I stumble
out of rooms 6923 toward breakfast. John Berryman
is there like Giotto, blue and gold,
announcing his downfall. What can I say to Deng Jing
and my class about why Berryman left the clinic and jumped
    from a Minnesota bridge
onto the frozen Mississippi?

2

As on other winter days I hop on my pumped-up green Flying
    Pigeon,
breeze through the guards at the north gate
where I'm blown by Gobi dustwinds out on the boulevard
among mules and shitwagons. I sweat congealed
as I rehearse my talk, dodge trucks roaring by like war
under the masked riders of heaven, Dao and De,
run down the stinking corridor to my classroom,
the icebox.

3

No one of us pulls off clothing. I'm up on a platform,
sit facing a microphone, head stuffed in my scarf.
I shiver and lecture almost blind. Wind-ghosts audit
outside the unsealed windows.
Someone has honored me by placing a thermos bottle
by the lectern; hot water heats my throat
while I cough up a month-old puddle of infection.

4

During break we walk in the courtyard sun
to shake off frost of our unlighted shabby class.
Thawing out I think what can I say to you, Deng Jing,

about an American poet at the peak of fame
who sharpened his pen and spat saliva
on his dreadful banker father's grave.

5

A few of us drift after class to the bike lot.
Talked out with Mistress Bradstreet, I recall
the scandalous evening at our school underground shelter
    dance
when we left together to chat about the important things.
You were criticized by the student leader
but you shouted him down and shamed him.

6

Now you disappear and return like the phoenix tree.
One day we'll all be with Mao pushing up masses
    of daisies.
Your words. To me you are like nomadic swan geese,
flying out of Shanghai.
Don't worry. Tonight we'll sit close to the stage
while the provincial opera company
sings falsetto in Mandarin dress and leaps into cartwheels,
whirling shiny wooden swords.
Don't worry about the madness of those patients
screaming in the Shanghai hospital where your uncle
    works,
or the destiny of some U.S. poets
since we, and especially you, have years before we join
    John Berryman
walking under his terrible water out to the island.

Paris Is Clearer Tonight

1

Wu, you studied abroad, were infected by the West,
were accused of being the three heinous "antis":
anti-people, anti-party, anti-socialist.
So they sent you to Chinese Siberia to remold you,
which you said was OK, you enjoyed it, but really
they didn't remold, only punished during 58 to 61,
the famine years,
and when you were starving they let you go.
Who wanted to be stuck with the corpse of a stinking
        intellectual?

2

Zhou Jueliang, wise Mandarin friend, in the morning
you gave me two facsimile volumes of Wang Wei
from a rare Song volume,
but dear Jueliang, after you wrote that fine piece
on "Ode to the West Wind"
(and Chairman Mao said clearly the East Wind triumphs
        over the West Wind),
they paraded you in a dunce cap while you beat a drum,
forced to yell *wo shi yige zhichanjieji fenzhi!*
        "I am a bourgeois renegade!"
Didn't those burning middle school Red Guards
recall Marx's favorite poet, yes, Shelley?

3

So we eat and remember. You both remember Chicago
of the 40s and I remember Paris, l'Hôtel du Portugal
        et de Lisbonne,
where we went to sketch in the Luxembourg,
heard stories from Citroën, my Dutch buddy,
who hid five years in a basement from the Gestapo.

After so many years of mad authorities,
it's nice to overeat, drink something stronger
and more deliciously foul than maotai,
and safely tell old stories of the death
of a peasant emperor and his gang
or of your peasant savior in the camp.

4

I witness but you are actors in those global rites
where men with grand ideas and iron gums munch
        your liver.
You survive while the old bullies suffer indigestion
and look haunted and annoyed.
Zhou, you still ride your bike out to Beda,
Wu, you limp bounding over to lift the dinner table,
and brooding Citroën, big stringbean of a blond
        romantic Dutchman
who sold yellow poetry mags in Paris streets,
you hang on as the young man, nothing more.

5

Paris is clearer tonight, its cold slate roofs
walk home with me on Rue Jacob,
Paris is with me as we descend into winter,
walk under the concrete moon, freeze to the freezing bus,
        reliable 332,
yet I am still warm from the Canon flash
as we all posed, an hour ago in the outskirts
on the brick prairie of Beijing where in your safehouse
upstairs we all held our smile.

A Few Miles from Laos

I go from village to village, an outsider
looking for truth. It's a friendly morning
    to find nothing.
In the temple the newly made Buddha doll
dominates under its fresh orange paint.
I'm looking. It smiles forever saying nothing.
Artillery booms from the border.
Clouds and a mountain of silk cotton trees
move upsidedown in the glassy rice water.

There are no Hans in this Dai village.
During the Great Cultural Revolution
they ripped out the faces of the Buddha
but new faces are back on altars with newly woven
    prayer streamers.
Dai women are thin as bamboo.
They wear peacock sarongs, silver belts and white
    straw hats,
even when working barefoot in the fields.
Pigs lumber, nosing for food
before the rebuilt temple
where young saffron monks are playing cards.
I've no idea who was the master of the old master
in his kingdom on the bench,
who smokes his bamboo pipe while scrawling
a Hinayana prayer in Tibetan script.

Paddy water is a mirror for pristine forests.
The water buffalo, meandering, drop huge blops
of shit on the priestly road.
Again the thud of heavy guns. The Hans
and Vietnamese are still killing each other
    at the border.
I go from village to village, looking
for a translation of things into thought.

I wonder what two morning moths have in mind,
chasing over the cabbage.
Paddy water is a mirror
but without words to inform.
The sunny morning lasts two hundred years.

Flight to Rangoon

1

Long ago I became the shadow—though I try to live
    furiously.
I become the darkness on a page
since with each disaster, each insult to peace
    and maturity,
with each failure comes a shadow, and from the shadow
come words holding dusk and breakfast,
women and the abstract sanctuary of human union.
They brood me into a theater of remorse,
dance me up to the princely sun,
slip into my bed with its unremembered dreams
where I wander in Asia.

2

I'm in Burma for the week allowed
and gave two roses to the black Buddha
                         on Mount Popa
and received a spoonful of watermelon
from a small girl whose face was wholly painted
in tanaka against prickly heat.
She put her arm around my waist. I put mine
on her shoulder. Before I got back
in our truck, she laughed at my heart.

3

Monks in wine-colored robes,
intense behind their eyeglasses,
sit with their begging bowls, smoking at the corner
    tea house,
waiting like all the world.
The Buddha found peace and truth, say the Pali
    texts;

he gave up hunger and possessions.
Moving from shadows to ordinary longing,
I give up only time, and reluctantly.

4

But if I stay on in this monastery
whose white stupas rise over the cane fields,
if I stay seven years or till I die
and never leave this closed country,
nor send word outside,
the absence of one shadow of a shadow will stir
      no one.
Yet out of cowardice I can't escape into quietude
      and forget.
I leave words to nobody perhaps,
yet I am them again, even tonight
as I come back from the teak and cherry uplands,
looking through village after village.

5

Sitting past midnight in near darkness
on a chair alone by the wall,
I see the waiter pushing an empty dishcart
through a marble dining hall.
There is no one else in the Inle Room
of the rundown pleasant Hotel Mandalay,
no one or nothing
but one mosquito—and the shadow, mine, that I see
      poorly
on paper, that sustains me and takes my life.

Spirit Has a Beginning

Although there's no Director of the Scenes,
working especially for me, I bet
what happens is for good. Forgot my jeans
in Hong Kong; on a marble hill in Crete
I left a lens. Yesterday in Nepal
a boy got my glasses. Why do I lose
my things? Alms to the cosmos? When I fall
in love, it lasts a life, but I confuse
my lover, lose her, and walk for years
on fire. It's good. Rain will surprise my heart
one day before I die. Theologies
despise possessions, and while I feel no tears
for things, lost love rehearses death. Yet these
words come because I lose. Loss is a start.

The Great Wall of China

Most of the Long Wall—as the Chinese call it—
    is a ruin
and almost as old as Plato's beard.
In walking in the north I see it suddenly
crawling into a poplar valley,
flashing through turquoise fall.
On a hill it has gold rings like the fingers of a god
    in armor.
It spreads as a great river
of stone against Mongols and Manchus—beautiful
as a sunflower, and useless.

Another wall, of equal grandeur, snakes around my hotel
    and university,
snooping outside the huts of strangers in the hutongs
and next to friends in their guarded flats.
It is ugly
and sinister as an informer's notebook.
Often—even in the raw sun battling into the haze
    over polluted cities—
it is invisible,
and like scorpions in shoes or rats on their chest
my friends in blue coats fear it.

On rare days when the Secret Long Wall is merely a ruin
sterile and dried up by the moon,
you my closest friends persist in seeing its watchtowers
    and telescopes
as an astrologer sees gold typhoons blowing among
    planetary rings.
On these benign days, I phone you,
but you fear passing through its gate to my room
as if you were still Mongols and Manchus, Tibetans
    or Uigurs
outside the stone eyes of the dreamt-up dragon.

The wall is heavy, omniscient, everywhere
so your feet are tattooed and turned to stone,
and I'm like you—foolish, cowardly, sane and streetwise.
Who can walk against the Great Invisible Wall?

Jiang Yuying, Famous Professor at Beijing University,
Who Daringly Rendered into Chinese the First Complete
Walt Whitman

1

Yuying, you have more spontaneous sting in you
than all the hot pepper in Nepal.

2

The Red Guards humiliated your scholar husband
and he hanged himself
but when they beat you with a leather strap
one hundred times and shaved your head,
you turned loose a galloping horse of ice
in the hidden stadium of a crystal word.
You laughed at them.
How could they make *you* look like a Chinese nun?

3

You survive to tell China truths. Afraid? Was Whitman,
the boisterous fully contradictory Walt Whitman
in seed-picker outfit, a coward?
Whitman took the Fulton Street Ferry up to his bohemian bar,
Pfaffs, where he held court
or in his red shirt, open at the front, rode all over
his Manhattan on the open bus.
He kissed and wrote letters for a wounded soldier
in a Virginia hospital,
and nursed his slow brother Ed whom he lived with.
Yuying you are a friend
of the amorous freemouthed deviant who sang himself.

4

The Guards whipped your theologian father.
He was 86.

He carted his own bags down to the countryside
where they sent him to remold his mind.
It's too late, you say, what can they do now to you,
     an old lady?
(Yet why have I made up a name for you, Yuying?)

5

In bad years young fanatics always rise to denounce
     the wicked,
roaring slogans like their statued fathers,
yet, Yuying, you wait them out with humor.
You are loquacious
and candid on your own piece of grass
like the old bearded failure with his disciples
at his bedside.

6

Now, you have made Whitman Chinese,
that American gray saint who looks in the mirror
at his ravaged eyes and mouth.
Of course he gazes at you with satisfaction,
Mandarin Camarado, hurting, surviving,
soon for darkness and loth to depart,
and announces an end that shall lightly and joyfully
     meet its translation.
He sees the problematic poet who will die in 1892
in Camden, New Jersey,
a loner in his respectable poor man's room,
garrulous like you to the very last.

Lunch with Maomao, Tubercular Translator of Sylvia Plath

This morning you recite some lines
of Sylvia Plath. I am so moved.
"And I eat men like air." The pines
in poems of Wang Wei have proved
his empty mountains are my friend,
yet I can't say them in your tongue.
You give me trees to eat, and blend
this May with eggs. But I'm a child
today, illiterate, and see
a black fish in your eye. It's mild
down in the poison sea. My plea
to sun is burn down in your lung
so you can finish Plath. Then brash
and cured, you both will rise from ash.

Convict Blue and Gray

In each small city, until London Fog raincoats,
Italian jackets and heeled boots take over,
herds of people ride plump bikes, hang out

in offices, walk the streets in convict
blue and gray. It is drab. It is tedious
like the Russian teardrop lamp bowls on

every lamppost. I want to get out of China
and abandon friends. But I recall Chou Ping
in his Chinese blue, writing an elegy for

13 black saxophones. What does your father do?,
I asked this morning. "He's a common carter
in a factory." Or when Jie left today,

on the stairway she said maybe next year
she could see me in another country and speak
freely. It is base. The new buildings are

slumscrapers. The old cadres are snoopy
and stupid and brutal to the young. Stores
are all the same, with ugly cheap junk,

nothing works and wait and *This is China*
my Chinese friends say, and I could vomit
because I love them and I'd put my life

in their hands, since like no one else
my friends are gentle, generous, teasing,
and candid like lovers on their pillow,

courageous in a land where each old tile
or embracing persimmon tree is a mystery
visible along with gray and blue convict

ghosts moving patiently in the streets.

In the Mansion of Confucius, and in the Cemetery Park of His Descendants Where I Rented a Horse and Lost Something

1

April has come. Blue sun. The pipa lute throbs
through the loudspeaker. Peasants bused in from farms
to walk through and gape at the mansion
gather round me in the courtyard to watch
me write. They glare. I am more a curiosity
than the plump Han warrior statue guarding
the entrance. I must be a stone relic.

Confucius also sat here, revising 305 poems
of *The Book of Poetry*. Was he wise?
Would Plato have picked him apart in a tricky dialogue?
But dull Plato was a mule, tossing poets into
    the street.
After a worshipful century in the grave
the Chinese sage ceased to be ordinary,
yet Confucius wasn't to blame that his disciples
made him holy and built him temples
or turned his virtue into fortune cookies.

When alive he grew nimble by a pine tree
with scrolls he wrote out for literate kings.
While Lao Tzu juggled stars
and voyaged to the world's beginning,
Confucius sat outside in the flowery courtyard
(ignoring Lao Tzu's misty inward power)
and played with ancient harmonies. Like a mule
he held to the boring wisdom of duty and goodness.

2

Afternoon, in the vast cemetery
where thousands of descendants of Confucius rot

70

in their pits. I wrote about the paper flowers
wind-torn on the mounds, a blue boy
with big Buddha ears, the grand cypresses
over first spring violets. In a notebook
I scribbled about the lovely peace,
about the aging Confucian, Tu Fu, with his daughter,
	lamenting exile,
whose sufferings inked his brushpen.
Then cantered on a blond horse.
Some place in the cemetery
as I trotted through the woods
the red notebook with the poem dropped from my pocket.
This is the ghost I am rewriting,
remembering almost nothing. It is best.
Loss is always best.
In the cemetery, what peace is greater than the oblivion
	of descendants
number 73 and 74, under their mounds
with torn paper flowers and unpondering violets,
in an evening green with its own memory?

Far South Mountain Cottage

In my middle years I love the Tao
and by Far South Mountain I made my home.
When happy I go alone into the mountain.
Only I understand this joy.
I walk until the water ends, and sit
waiting for the hour when clouds rise.
If I happen to meet an old woodcutter,
I chat with him, laughing and lost to time.

Wang Wei (701–761)
translated by TB, WB, XH

Pilgrim Road

1

The sun and moon float together at daybreak
over the windy summit of Taishan, the Holy Mountain.
I lived one month on the Holy Mountain
     at Agion Oros.
The Greek army was still fighting stray guerrillas
in the snows of the forested peninsula,
but not even ghosts of the Tartar rebels
are a threat to the Jade Emperor.

2

People climb the most sacred peak in China.
Hundreds of old ladies with bad tiny feet
     and black velvet hats
pass through the red gate and stop at the first
     Taoist temple
to prostrate themselves before
the local clothed bronze goddess.
They flame a piece of paper before the tiny shoes
     on the altar
and toss small coins on it
between the candles and incense.

3

Candles and incense filled the cave of the Theologian,
writing his Book in Patmos.
For two years John lived on the island with his Revelations
and seven white whales circling on the sea
below his white hill village.

4

Wind at the summit of Taishan fiercely slaps
old men in black padded trousers

and couples posing next to calligraphed steles
where they become immortal
in the lenses of dinky Sea Gull cameras.
Wind almost blows me off the rock bridge.
The sun and moon kiss their own sides of heaven.
I pass through the moongate,
follow a rocky path where lovers left bottles,
where a smell of shit was souped up by the gale.

5

When I left Patmos on a small caique, hugging the bowrail,
the *meltemi* almost blew me off the helmsman's deck.
Wind ecstatically kicked up the icon-blue water
     between the islands.
The Cave of the Apocalypse was already stuck for good
in my head. Pilgrim steps of Taishan
are already becoming memory.
With the old women with tiny feet prostrate before
the bronze goddess of the mountain
and porters crazy-eyed balancing 90 beers on their pole
     up to workers' bars,
with Chinese sand-wind beating into my unholy eyes
and the summit circling, swaying under the radar tower
     and sunrise boulders
I look far below at faint white
spring in the valley. Time freezes. I never descend.

III   *5 Spring Songs in China, and Trashcart Mule*

The Tree of Life

Don't cry for me. The Tree of Life
is full of birds. When I was old
in winter, lonely as a knife,
and when my heart was blue and cold,
I fell in love. Don't cry for me.
The Tree of Life is lilac blue
and smells of May and poverty,
poor as an orchard of bamboo.
I fell in love when I was young
and now I'm crazy once again,
in jail with jasmine on my tongue
and in my heart a cyclamen.
Don't cry for me. I'm young again
and every spring is cyclamen.

Spring Is

Spring is. I guess my life is still
a glance at resurrection. I've had
my share of winter. With no will
or fear at all, I eased from sad
and hollow to your Burmese thighs
slender and frank like the new moon,
and wondrous. When I kissed your eyes
of darkness, I knew sun, a noon
of accident. We plan. Spring is,
though you have flown off to a cave
to look at paintings. "I will miss
you," and you went. A season gave
us life. I wonder: Are we found
or lost? It's dawning underground.

Overcast

Look in your soul, O love. It's green,
and overcast and raining there,
its cows float up from a ravine.
You see as far as everywhere.
Be still. Look in your soul. Be still
inside as Adam's sleep, and hear
your hobo eyes under a hill
of dream. The dirty spring is here,
the Beijing alleys overcast,
a hutong court of memories.
You look for home. Strangely a past
of barn, of island and Greek seas
shows in the rain. I share your bowl
of mist. It's raining in your soul.

Season of Falling out of Stars

Spring takes a year and then it hurts
because I'm incomplete, which is
how you feel too. I let my shirts
pile up, swear I'll wash them, yet fizz
away like coke, can't clean up. For
some other time I say and dive
behind a book down on the floor.
I flop but Oh you're still alive
and I'm alive. Blood on the snow,
carbombs and a Tibetan shot
mumbling a prayer but you are not
a TV ghost. How prison slow
your coming was! My love for you
dresses a gulag in nice blue.

A Bell in the Deep Mountain

Dante was right to ignore heaven
and put Francesca in her Hell
of doves, young and not after seven
decades. Love, being the deep bell
in the wood, only rings on earth,
our glory Hell, not in the sky.
We feel an unseen love at birth.
Then walk a day alone, and die
to no lucent Inferno but
to nothing. Dante envied her,
her paradise. I want that hut
of one shared universe, her fir
tree on a mountain. Cast in shade,
I cast for bells before I fade.

Trashcart Mule

As I near my schoolgate, just another worker
on my bicycle, used to dodging death,
sharp in sniffing out coal from dung in drizzling rain,
late again yet proud of being Chinese,
I pass an upturned trashcart
and brake because its mule is waiting stiff,
a splattered statue,
garbage hanging on it like rippings from an ancient
     codicil.
The driver on his knees, sweeping, ordinary
in his hurry to amend, ignores the small crowd.
I can't stay to watch
but the incident is perfectly serious. It is
a chronicle of minor calamity
and a test of moderation. I leave the small crowd for duty.
The incident is closed,
no time to see the resolution and cleanup
of the animal and street,
of the resurrected driver and his patient mule,
its eyes bulging yellow with sun,
trash hanging on its black hair like wasted garments
from the mighty Qin Shi Huangdi.
Standing half naked, mere staring mule,
it is more alive
than all the emperor's terra cotta generals and stallions,
dug up and exposed,
who glare straight ahead in eternal boredom
from their dusty open tomb at Chang'an.

Xian Incident

Poor Xian, cold and stinking in winter like Buffalo's
    southside factories.
Its people walk in convict blue through pollution
    grayness.
Its black market con men
loaf around the railroad station.
City of a Yellow Emperor and his terra cotta army
in mountainous tombs.
Xian is old Chang'an, city of Tang Illumination
where court poets sang for ladies
of a meditating hermit in the pine mountain.

After being hassled for hours down at the reception
    desk,
I got so sore I threw a flowerpot out the window
of the People's Hotel. The police threatened
but could prove nothing.
Ravaged Xian, bulldozed like monasteries and spirit
    of Tibet,
ugly new city of unwalkable long blocks.
Only the old tangled Muslim quarter is alive
at night with outdoor markets, oil lamps and smell
    of roasted mutton.

Around Xian is the longest city wall in China,
made of austere moon-bricks,
around a sky-mirror moat.
Inside, the new city's four models of prefabs fade
    in acid fumes,
itching in the mysterious mist of coal smoke.
Trucks pound the streets
with workers sleeping like toads on their loaded beds.
Ming Wang was the Brilliant Emperor,
poet and patron of Tang glories
in a nation of singing birds

till the Tartar general rebelled the city into
    chaos.
The police bluffed but let us go.
Wretched Xian, like Buffalo it stinks in winter.

Written in the Mountains in Early Autumn

I'm talentless and dare not inflict myself on this
    bright reign.
Perhaps I'll go to the East River and mend my old fence.
I don't blame Shang Ping for marrying off his children early;
rather, I think Master Tao Yuan Ming left office too late.
With a cricket's cry autumn abruptly falls
    on my thatched hall.
The thin haze of evening is saddened with the whine
    of cicadas.
No one calls. My cane gate is desolate.
Alone in the empty forest, I have an appointment
    with white clouds.

Wang Wei (701–761)
translated by TB, WB, XH

Under the Great Iceberg

I guess under the iceberg is more ice
or maybe deep in the water is fire
as below my Beijing cheerfulness a gloomy
pilgrim circles like a diseased bat.
The bat darts 30 years around its temple.
Most of China lies under the ocean.
                    +
After a year on the yellow continent
I put my papers in a mound—no order here—
work at these books through another night,
then try for home. Where is it now?
Wherever I go China disturbs, incites,
and beyond each mountain lies a mountain.
                    +
I guess under the iceberg is more ice,
and most of China lies under the ocean.
Her epithets confuse me: Deng Jing,
People's Republic, Wang Meng, Cathay.
These names are no metaphors. Under
the ocean in China I feel the fire.

Crooked Planet

a

In those secret books when Jews and Gnostics
were still looking in Egypt for the messiah.
I liked to read about heaven
with patriarchs in white dazzling raiments,
gold houses on clouds, sapphire eyes of sages
gazing through a snow of diamonds,
walls built of tessellated crystals with tongues of fire.
But life up there, its eternal days all the same,
isn't such a vision a bore?

b

On earth I spend an hour after sweet rain
outside the village of Yangshuo. We came down from
Moon Hill, exhausted.
Plain rain. Trucks exploding down the road, horns
bellowing, cease.
Only a few women poling quickly down the paths
with pails of shit-water for the rice fields.
The smell disappears a while. Then a rainbow
winks over the sky, imitating paradise.
The rainbow wisely endures only a few minutes.
I leave, letting it glow eternally
from gray huts to receding peaks.

c

The sun is rolling from peak to crooked peak
as it descends.
It imitates a hot-lighted yellow moon.
Then drops away, behind Crab Hill,
sleepwalking toward the Americas.
Back in my hotel a glass rose with a bulb inside
declares itself bright,
but its electrical spirit withers and goes black.

d

I'm flying now from city to city. Heaven lies
above the cabin window.
Everyone has been looking: all those old men,
Antony in Egypt (as young Cavafy remembered him),
who went to the window
and listened with pleasure and courage
to the strange music passing in the street
while he waited for morning doom.

e

I'm not different. But I look back,
with you, from a bridge,
pondering crooked limestone mountains backing
into mist. China imitates China.
In those secret books
I think I hear toads that sat outside my window,
yesterday, when I couldn't think at all,
who sat and spoke to the indifferent pagoda
on the crooked peak overlooking poor elegant bamboo.
Suddenly it rains on that stand
of green pleasure
which love scratches forever in our forgetting.

My Daughter Aliki Coming to China

a

O the thousand rooms of the Forbidden City,
its red walls around imperial courts leading
endlessly into other gigantic marble courts
or, as if by grace or intuition, into one
intimate garden with great pine trees and a small gold
    and blue temple,
all that I've not gone back to. I'm saving them
for you. That labyrinth—once of concubines,
jewels and Yellow Emperors where now old women
in gray trousers squat in the shadow of Ming yellow
    tile roofs—
I keep intact for us.

b

Will you leave Chinatown and the Mission for a Buddha
in the cave? The mist of Tang poems
among the factories is a bit noxious
but late spring is sweet with your arrival
and every leaf outside my room is a pond of sun
in which crickets cry out in four tones.
Do you remember how we found that window sign in Madrid
saying CUBAN CHINESE FISH
and we took a room and laughed down the streets
of Lope and Quevedo? Lope and Li Po,
scholars say they had almost the same bohemian
madness.

c

Come as soon as you can. I'll be at the airport
with motorcycle, chopsticks, a bag of books,
and we'll be as if wandering Spanish streets again,
wake each morning as children among slogans
near old men sitting outside with caged birds;

and on a rare afternoon of rain in Beijing
we'll hear the smell of lilac trees
blazing perennial in the courtyard by the doorway.

d

Whitman, expert in rebirth, knew all about Chinese
        beginnings.
We'll start in the streets of the night market
under oil lamps
with Uigurs yelling at us to buy kebab.
Can you smell Chinese June in San Francisco?
From our foreigners' compound and infamous gate
I already taste our walk up Fragrant Mountain,
or the oncoming blue of street crowds
or the smoky wind in public buses.

e

At the north gate of the Forbidden City
are great stone dogs, a rose garden, and a long moat
with rowboats dozing on gold water
between the palace wall and poor huts. There,
one late afternoon, men hanging out in undershirts
will look at us as we trail by.
Children will drop their arms and stare curiously
until we are gone. Then in my rooms,
we'll talk away our evening on Xinjiang rugs,
by maps and oil lamps,
in a labyrinth of unforbidden friends.

*IV   With Uigurs in the Gobi Desert
and Tibetans on the Roofland*

A Nomad Camp in the Gobi

Off the road near Turfan, where the Gnostics sought
escape from the body,
escape from the lowest pocket on the planet
to the Realm of Light,
the desert nomads have a camp. Up in Tibet
(just a thousand miles south)
the nomads on the roofland by the sky lakes
have one reader in the morning chanting sutras
for the others. He sits on a slope
rocking as he sings to other lives.
Here, the wandering Turks turn five times a day
to Mecca, boil turnips, talk to strangers
(which I can't understand)
like me whom they insist on drowning
with hot dark water in their jars of tea.

Aliki Lost in Turkistan

1

By the rose and blue mosque
in the Kashgar open market
we go our ways to meet in an hour.
You look for rugs. I'm off for the row
of outdoor barbers who are shaving heads,
for bookstalls with old Korans calligraphed
in Arabic, Parsi,
with bright drawings.
Each leatherbound volume has a gold circle,
a time mirror of wars and migrations,
of conversions and a green minaret
wailing in Turkistan sandland.
I haggle an hour for a book. Walk off,
come back, forget our date, buy you a necklace
like a Mayan wedding strand I once saw
of big irregular pearls
scooped out of the sea off Quintana Roo.
By the time I bring you bible and pearl
you're gone. I've lost you.

2

Back in the alleys, children and women squat
by carved doorways, playing cards.
Alleys are a strategy of ancient mud walls.
Songs float out of windows. Incense floats.
Turkic chant hangs over the eye
of central Asia, its innermost city.
From the austere labyrinth, intricate and deep
    as a fossil,
I burst into the bazaar, searching through dresses,
cheap clocks and iron ladles.
Over the huge market a stone figure of Mao,
dead god vast in his starless overcoat,

commanding still.
He is no help at all. I pass the knife racks.
I ask the rug dealer if he has seen you.
I ask the hatwoman if she has seen you.
Ask foreigners. They all saw you pass by.
They don't lie. They're not watchmen of the towers
who beat the wandering Shulamite
looking for her love, sick with love, O sisters
     of Jerusalem!
My daughter is somewhere in this desert city
among the almond nuts and piles of red spice,
curry, coffee, moonbeans, baskets of freshwater
     pearls.
I rush off again through Sunday crowds.

3

At the horse market, ants work away
at plum peels in the mud puddles.
Kazakhs in fur hats and black corduroys
rock through in donkey carts jammed
with black goats.
Lambs lounge, legs tied, for their last day
on earth.
Their eyes are hangout eyes.
Han police and cadres are not around.
We are scarcely in China.

4

A lead comes in. You're in the textile street.
I beeline, ignoring the first logs of light
of the hatchet-faced moon,
ignoring white beards in white robes
near their animals and kebab smoke.
Tongue stuck to my teeth,
I stop to eat a melon. It's late. You could be anywhere:
in clear air near Pakistan,

in the tombs of Abaq,
or climbing villages, old as Sumeria, on the snow
mountain Kongur,
or jumping a waterditch to reach the Muslim cemetery
shaped by Cycladic geometers.

5

I never find you. The sky took you
to live in a crystal riverboat.
At the airport our plane motor is busted.
It's desert. We wait like lizards for the Russian aircraft
to move its rusted wings.
At the near horizon is a far mosque,
its eyeball dome blurring crosseyed into the Asia wind.
Wind of the Gobi.
In my childhood I swam in a Maine lake.
There was no sign of women in green veil cloths
tossed back on their shoulders
or carbon Flaming Hills or black pebble flatlands.
I eat one last bread ring. The baker spits on it,
polishes it on his shirt.

6

We play with continents on our fingers.
It's been a year of illusion.
I'll look for you next in Turfan,
oasis and frying pan of heavy air,
where Manichaeans ruled and Nestorians prayed.
In the lowest city of our planet,
maybe you are drinking grape wine in an arbor
or writing notes in your bed near the reeking toilet
in the Old Russian Consulate.
I'll look for you. My waterjug is empty.
It is eleven o'clock and still light
but you're not here.
I take a horsecart to my room to read.

7

Tomorrow in a small river through the Gobi
we'll splash in and cool off, ecstatically
at peace.
Childhood never leaves time.
Even the moon has childhood memory
as it enters the darkening mountains of stones.
Even now in Gobi sun
where we sweat out another lost plane
outside the airport shrieking its banal songs,
or earlier today
when we ate a pyramid of cakes with Mishram
in his rug-filled Uigur room,
you are there, childhood there eternally,
unless, fishing out worry glasses, I look up
and find you gone.
We play with continents.
A daughter has her own ancient cities,
her palace exploding with words,
her books of time that are a few times
my corner of rain falling on the neighborhood
with its smells.
Now gone from Kashgar, even Xinjiang, maybe China,
you are not lost.
Next summer we take a walk to the *fournos*
for the evening bread
or meet at the lettuce store on white Odos Perseus
or take the gravel road winding up toward
the high monasteries in the mountains of Serifos.
Each year we are nomads
in the politics of love.

Here in Xinjiang there are less riots; insiders talk
of reconciliation between Turks and Hans
but the Uigurs carry knives.
I saw six furious Turks in Muslim velvet caps kick a Han
to an inch of his life.

Childhood never leaves time.
Even the moon has childhood memory
as it enters the darkening mountains of stones
where we drift
permanently lost and find a way.
Late at night you find your way back
to the outdoor granite table and our moldy room
at the lyrical Old Russian Consulate.
Tomorrow in a small river through the Gobi...

Fire over Tibet

Tibet is cloud and vulture high, and its air so thin
we are still too dizzy to stand.
In Cuzco it took me four days before I could walk
in the Inca capital.
Here I throw up greasy noodles
that I ate in the Muslim shop
and wobble slowly up to bed.

*

Five Han police burst into my room. Midnight,
I'm sleeping and think flowerpots.
The Tibetan cleaning woman stands behind them,
      making faces.
These thin men in loose green laundry bags leave.
No worry. Only a passport check.
In a few days I'll have enough oxygen in my blood
to walk into the hills.

*

Village houses are low rectangles of mud.
Saint John of the Cross said the soul
is a bird on a string, straining for heaven.
Each cairn and rooftop has a swarm of Buddhist prayer
      flags
tied on sticks, flying upward into a theology
      of low clouds.
Each village has a dynamited monastery.

*

This morning there is festival in the few monasteries
      not blown up.
Clouds smelling of hash float out of the gold roofs
of the Jokhang.
Pilgrims circle this ancient sanctuary
in whose courtyard so many got the bullet

in the back of the neck.
These days it's hard to love China.

*

Tibet is mountains and luminous fields
        fresh and green
as northern Maine.
Shadow and fire shine on this gentle people
who laugh and touch you,
on Kampas in the mountains still fighting like Afghans
for liberation.

*

Scant atmosphere.
Lakes lie breathless by fields of yellow mustard;
herbs and wildflowers have quick summer life.
A caravan in native rags appears on the gravel
        road.
Coral faces, leather faces, turquoise in their ears.
We shake hands, poke each other. The caravan goes off
along this beautiful wasteland.
These nomads and their goats on the meager
        exhilarating grass
somehow survive.
Overhead, the sun is a violet-fire blowtorch.

A Dream of My Father in Tibet

1

Father, thirteen years are gone since Canton,
the hotel room, the dream where we last met.
Again you show up in China. Or is Tibet China?
We are waiting for a bus to come to Gyangze
I worry how you will take the snow passes—
not much to breathe at 18,000 feet.
For the first time I suppose you looking old
(as if 40 years since your death could have aged you)
in a flannel suit, bright blue tie, gold watch chain
and shoes polished.
Or am *I* older in my third-world traveler outfit?

2

My children are here to meet you
(they never knew you, since you leapt away before
    their birth).
Mother's here too—blond against the snow.
Should we put you both in the same room?
You arrive. Respectable, against bluish fields.
No, I say,
we were always wrong and crazy together.
In a flash you change, a kid in Boston subways,
selling newspapers, buying a nickel-beer lunch.
Then I'm twelve and we're at the Met
before a Rembrandt. You talk dreamily about
    the "genius"
who painted a beggar as a Polish nobleman.

3

We climb drunk on fine air to the top of the huge mountain
    fortress
Gurkhas once stormed into for the British.
Stone whale dominating Gyangze.

Scaling wall upon wall, breathless, we ascend
into the sky,
As we climb you tell me the alphabet of night,
begin to say who you are, who I am,
how you show up when you are dead...
but the wood plank under the thin mattress
bangs into my hipbone. I wake, go out in the dark
to take a leak.
It's brightly cold before dawn!

4

The old half moon has dulled the Milky Way
just over the truck stop. Stumbling
on my way outside to the foul toilet house,
I realize you are escaping again!
Will I live to find you once more in China?
I freeze back to my room, digging through mind
        to spot you
in incomplete dream, in dream becoming unremembered.
Am I using you for your secrets, my young father?

5

Tibet of relentless beauty in mountains,
of stone ghosts—once monasteries—meditating
over every village hill,
of colorful cartoon universes on tankas,
of silk banners hanging in shadowy temple chambers,
we see them together. You are my shadow companion.
Will you come back? I am impatient, deprived
        of our explorations.
Let no one know. We can meet obscurely,
perhaps in Bolivia again.
No one in the Andes will notice.
Alone we are confused; together we eat wonderful
bottled apples.

6

Although you are buried again in the sky, behind clouds
        startlingly clean,
above mustard fields on the earth's highest plateau,
I wear you as a water bottle in these carbon and orange
        mountains,
I wear you as red coral on the outside of my heart,
I wear you as a watch chain before sunrise
along with beads and a few pens on my shirt.

Walking out of China

1

After the dreaded customs
where I wear my university badge on my shirt pocket
and slip through as a respectable teacher,
we descend from the altiplano,
dropping dangerously down through no-man's-land.
Mist fills the ravines. Tibet behind us,
the lower hillsides are traditional Chinese painting.
A glassy stream wiggles below in the throat of
    huge gorges.
A rhododendron forest is a temple of nature gods
and shadows.

2

As shacks of Nepal and the Friendship Bridge
appear at the bottom of deep rock clefts,
    my fever grows.
Poisoned on unboiled water,
and worse, ripped untimely from the Chinese womb
after just a year's immersion,
yet now I breathe sea level oxygen, fully free
to travel anywhere
with no permit from the Security Bureau.
Perhaps my brain is wild and curly
like the forest path. Stomach convulsed,
backpack overloaded, water gone, no food,
I drag through a divorce strip of nature between
    nations,
by the laughing Himalayas.

3

Walking out of China, burned out with bureaus
    and repression,
I am peacefully confused.

Exhilarated, fed up, turned into thief and liar,
I keep all my cards in my money belt:
white People's Money card, blue Work Unit card,
red Travel card, brown Eating card,
green Residence card,
ready to pull one out and shout murder at some
        hotel cadre
if denied "Foreign Expert" rates.
My nerves are raw. Yet it's years too soon to go.
Impossible to forget. I feel shock.

4

China is cabbage. China is the smell of urine
in the halls of my much loved *shueiyuan*
and in the new Boeing 727 invading Lhasa.
China is the morning loudspeaker screaming homilies
        in a Kashgar hotel yard,
waking us from uncollective dream.
Peasants, in every province, so many even a Baptist god
cannot count them.
But crowds are an abstraction.
I care for friends,
for the poets (we conspired every night in Beijing)
and Lu Jie whose voice is cello smooth,
who never shivered in the iciest winter restaurant
where we used the tablecloth as our blanket;
for Ye Junjian and his sumptuous modest meals:
the Cambridge novelist who scrubbed toilets
during the day and saved his mind at night
        for art.
When I left you, Junjian, I said (we were waiting
for a crowded bus, you in Mandarin vest)
I would not disappear like a ship in the gloom.

5

I wandered to China a few times.
There is no grave for memory, although Swedenborg said God

gave us a brain so we could forget. Yet a woman
is never gone, a nation never gone. So here
I am only half here, and obsessively return
to the yellow continent.
A moth's eyebrow invaded my liver—only the Chinese
    have such dreams—
and lights my insomnia with an owl's vision.
I mourn too much.
After all, a parent, a woman, even a nation
(father, lover, even China)
each has the human right to go off and be apart,
to rest or die a while alone.

6

Wang Wei had enough loss and went to the mountains
    to write his poems.
He heard an ancient bell.
As I walk out of China, confused, angry, lovesick,
the birds echoing in these gorges are obtuse to memory.
They merely cry about food and lust.
Through them I hear a bell in the deep mountain.
Through the calligraphic pines and vulture skies,
over the oxen stepping through deep mirrors
    in the paddies
of every unseen province,
over new doll-like Buddhas in dinky strange Dai temples
    up on stilts,
from the destroyed faces of family deities in Xinjiang
and plain Ming merchant homes in Anhuei,
from these winds fallen from Tibetan tablelands
    into classical Tang gorges,
from a visit by the same Buddhist painter-poet
    to the hermit in his forest
there comes a bell in the deep mountain.

"Going Back to China." Tu Fu (713–770), Tang dynasty poet. In the traditional Wade-Giles system, his name is transcribed Tu Fu, leading most readers to pronounce the initial *t* as *t*. In the Wade-Giles system *t* is actually pronounced *d* and only *t'* is pronouned *t*; hence in Wade-Giles, Tang dynasty is transcribed T'ang dynasty. I have followed *pinyin* for transcribing most of the Chinese names and words into the Roman alphabet. Some names, however, such as Tu Fu and Li Po, because they are still known to English readers primarily in Wade-Giles spelling, are left as Tu Fu and Li Po rather than pinyin Du Fu and Li Bai.

"5 A.M. in Beijing." "Xinjiang," meaning New Province, is the largest province in China. Located in the northwest, it was formerly called Chinese Turkistan. Its proper name today is the Autonomous Uigur Republic. Although there is now a large Han migration in the cities, the countryside is populated by Turkic Muslims: Uigurs, Kozakhs and Uzbekhs.

"Cycling Home on My Flying Pigeon." Flying Pigeon is the brand name of a Chinese bicycle.

"Snow." Wang Wei (701–761), Tang dynasty poet and painter.

"Walter Whitman." Walt Whitman was born Walter Whitman. Jorge Luis Borges has an excellent essay on Walt, the healthy figure created in the poems and Walter Whitman the man, the failure, who never went to the exotic places of his poetic atlas. This poem is about Walter. "Youyi Binguan" means Friendship Hotel. The large Friendship Hotel in Beijing, in the university district, was originally built by the Russians for Russians in China. When the Russians were expelled it was occupied by Albanians. It now houses "foreign experts," other guests and tourist groups.

"Brooding on Wangfujing Street." Wangfujing is a crowded, main shopping street in downtown Beijing.

"Seeing Zu Off at Qizhou." The translations from Wang Wei were done by Tony Barnstone, Xu Haixin and myself.

"Cristoforo Colombo." Sima Qian (2nd century–c. 85 B.C.) is China's first major historian, who wrote a volume of 132 chapters giving the entire history of China until his own time. He was castrated by the emperor Wu Di for having defended a prominent Chinese general who had been forced to resign after a defeat. Some of his work was considered more legendary than historical, such as the claim that Qin Shi Huangdi, who in the third century B.C. built the Great Wall and from whom the name China derives, was buried in a tomb with 10,000 clay soldiers. Recently, when Shi Huangdi's tombs were partially excavated near Xian, some 7,000 clay soldiers were found, and each year there are new finds.

"The Pungent Smell of China." Hypatia, philosopher and mathematician, last major Neoplatonic philosopher of Alexandria, was famous in part because of her barbarous murder by a band of Christian monks in A.D. 415. Part 3 is shamelessly modeled on the structure of "The God Abandons Antony" by the Alexandrian Greek poet Constantine Cavafy (1863–1933).

"Words on Rice Paper." Chengde is a small city five hours north of Beijing, with a Summer Palace for the Beijing emperors, and important temples, including Tibetan ones.

"Meeting Near the Summer Palace." The Yiheyuan is the Summer Palace. Youyi is short for Youyi Binguan, Friendship Hotel.

"At the Moscow Restaurant by the Zoo." " 'Down to the countryside' " is a euphemism for being sent to camps for "remolding" minds during the Cultural Revolution (1966–76).

"Reading Li Qingzhao." Li Qingzhao (1084?–1151?), Song dynasty woman poet.

"In a Beijing Monastery." After the Cultural Revolution (1966–76), some monasteries were again opened and monks allowed to return. The second monastery referred to, "White Cloud Temple," is Taoist.

"Going to Temples outside Chengde." See note on "Words on Rice Paper."

"China Moon." *Hanyu* means Chinese language or simply Chinese.

"Dreams and Memories on an Ordinary Evening / in a Russian-built Apartment." "Russian-built apartment" refers to the Youyi Binguan, the Friendship Hotel, built by the Russians. Vicente is the Spanish poet Vicente Aleixandre (1898–1984).

"Ways of January 2, 1985." Quevedo is the Spanish poet Francisco de Quevedo (1580–1645).

108

"Paris Is Clearer Tonight." Beda is short for Beijing Daxue, Peking University.

"A Few Miles from Laos." In semitropical Xixuabanna, in Yunnan Province. Dai refers to a Thai people living in China; in Burma the Thais are called Shans, from the word Siam.

"Flight to Rangoon." Mount Popa lies between Pagan and Mandalay. At the top is a Buddhist monastery.

"The Great Wall of China." Hutongs are old city alleys with small houses alongside them.

"In the Mansion of Confucius." Confucius (551?–479? B.C.). Lao Tzu (604?–531? B.C.), founder of Taoism.

"Pilgrim Road." The Theologian is John of Patmos, or John of Ephesos, the author of Revelation (the Apocalypse).

"Trashcart Mule." For more on Emperor Qin Shi Huangdi and Chang'an, see note on "Colombo." In ending this poem, I heard an echo—or stole one—from the ending of Sappho's poem to Anaktoria in which Sappho compares her love for Anaktoria to chariots and hoplites of Lydia:

> these things remind me now
> of Anaktoria who is far,
> and I
> for one
> would rather see her warm supple step
> and the sparkle of her face—than watch
> all the dazzling chariots and armored
>
> > hoplites of Lydia.

Translation is from my *Greek Lyric Poetry*, pp. 66–67.

"Xian Incident." Xian, south of Beijing, was old Chang'an, capital of Tang dynasty China.

"Written in the Mountains in Early Autumn." The poems in this collection appear largely in chronological order and follow the seasons of the year, beginning with late summer and fall to the end of the next summer. So the appearance of this poem, with "Autumn" in its title and text, would seem out of place in a section of late spring.

Perhaps it is. I put it there, however, rather than among the first poems, because apart from the season it seemed the right place.

"Crooked Planet." Yangshuo is a village a few hours by water south of Guilin.

"My Daughter Aliki Coming to China." Quevedo is Francisco de Quevedo (1580–1645), poet and novelist of the Spanish Golden Age. Lope is Lope de Vega (1562–1635), poet and playwright of the Spanish Golden Age. Li Po (701?–762), Tang dynasty poet.

"Aliki Lost in Turkistan." Kashgar in Xinjiang Province (Chinese Turkistan), the westernmost city in China, lies near the Pakistan border. It is a Uigur city, whose old central Asian buildings are still intact. Uigurs are Caucasian Muslims, speaking a Turkic language and related to Kazakhs and Uzbekhs, who also inhabit Xinjiang. The same peoples are found across the border in Russian Turkistan. Turfan, in the Gobi desert east of Urumuci, is the lowest city in the world. It was the capital city of Gnosticism, the state religion of Western China until the 12th century, when it was suppressed by Ghengis Khan.

"Fire over Tibet." The Jokhang is a major monastery in Lhasa.

Afterword

There are many Chinas, and this diversity marks the oneness of the Chinese spirit. In his introduction to George Seferis' *The King of Asine*, Rex Warner wrote that the Greek poet spoke not simply of an ancient and modern Greece but of many Greeces: Homeric, classical, Alexandrian, Byzantine, Turkish, revolutionary, modern, and in the many he saw the continuity of *romiosini*, the Greek spirit. So like Greece, China has many faces: the archaic Chin period of Qin Shi Huangdi, who gave China its name, unity and Great Wall, the Tang poets Tu Fu and Wang Wei at Chang'an, the Song dynasty elegance and pathos of Li Qingzhao, the Manchu dowager empress Ci Xi, cruel in her Summer Palace, and the peasant poet and Hunan emperor Mao Zedong.

*

When I was 20, in Paris, a student at the Sorbonne, I met Robert Payne, who had just returned from China. It was 1948 and the civil war was raging, but Payne, who had been in China five years, was enthusiastic about a poet he had met in a cave in northern China. Mao Tse-tung was his name (these were pre-pinyin days, before he became Mao Zedong). Payne had translated his poem "Snow" and other poems. He was the first to do a literary translation of some of the poems, and was soon to come out with an acerbic biography of the leader. In those days, however, he appeared interested only in the poetry. The next year Robert was the best man at my wedding in Paris.

In 1952–53 I went to study at the School of Oriental and African Studies at the University of London. I was especially interested in Tang and Song dynasty Chinese poetry, but I thought I would not get into China for 20 years. So I was a full-time student in Bengali, regretting it was not Chinese. Twenty years proved to be the time I was to wait to enter China, and that was early.

Robert Payne's words about the poet in the cave pursued me—he had also suggested that I work on Spanish poetry, and I began then to translate Antonio Machado, a life-long love and obsession. One afternoon in 1971, while walking in a parking lot at Indiana University, I turned on my heels and went to the library, where I found some dreary versions of Mao's poems. I wanted to translate the complete

poems. I proposed to work with Ko Ching-po, who would be an inform-
ant. Harper & Row published *The Poems of Mao Tse-tung* in a bilingual
edition, which included a study and extensive notes. It was a very
elegant Book-of-the-Month alternate selection, which the publisher
put out in 11 round-the-clock days when they discovered that a manu-
script they had had for six months was the poetry of the man Richard
Nixon was to see in a few days.

Meanwhile, I had been asked to go to China by Christopher Janus
and three other people from Chicago. I studied Chinese, made plans,
but no visa came through. In those days the Chinese simply did not
answer any requests for visas that came through normal channels.
Finally, I sent a wire that read, "Premier Chou Enlai, Peking, China.
I am the translator of the poems of Mao Tse-tung and would like to
visit China with four friends." By return wire came, "Go to Ontario,
Canada, to pick up your visas."

As the result of that unexpected wire from Beijing in late spring of
1972, I found myself suddenly in the Middle Kingdom, an observer
of a most unusual face of China. I spent my first night in Guangzhou
(Canton), and in the predawn heard military music wafting through
the balcony window. The periodic wind also carried in the thud of
soldiers double-timing in the streets. In the morning we found that
civilians were in austere blue military garb. Women had two permissible
hairstyles and could not wear dresses or skirts, even in summer. But
amid the drabness and suffocating black pollution of major cities, there
was paradoxically a fierce energy in Shanghai and a careful huge
splendor in Beijing. One evening in a private Beijing restaurant we
feasted on Peking duck in a four-hour ceremony, served by waiters in
western tuxedos. Outside, the Cultural Revolution was raging.

From the experience of that programed voyage came a book, *China
Poems,* in which I recalled what it was like to venture through an
unknown country. It was a personal book of a public, other world.
When I went back to the mainland 12 years later, there was again
another China. I returned as a teacher in a Beijing university. I had
my worker's blue and red cards, which permitted me to travel through-
out China without a passport, even to go to Tibet without special
permission. In that year there was also radical change in every aspect
of Chinese life and politics. Now, however, the informants were friends,

112

whom I would trust with my life. When at last given the limited freedom to be with "foreigners," the people I knew so well constantly moved me with their grace and candor. We were illegal together, we conspired, we loved, shared problems, meals, endless walks and journeys. I owe all that is essential in this book to these friends: poets, novelists, painters, professors and above all students, in class, and in my rooms or theirs where we collaborated in translating classical and contemporary Chinese poets into English. As opposed to the *almost* natural atmosphere of today let me remember the first trip to the new Middle Kingdom.

In May and June of 1972 I was in China. It was the sixth year of the Cultural Revolution. While the universities had reopened after being shut down for four years and ferocious factional warfare was over, millions of detainees lingered in prisons, in camps and the "countryside" where, our hosts informed us, their minds were being remolded. These were China's "stinking intellectuals" and those accused of rightist tendencies. In Tibet genocide persisted, and the destruction of more than 5,600 monasteries was enacted with furious ecstasy.

I went to China with love for its arts and people but at the same time was alerted against being brainwashed by slogans and the intensity of our hosts. It was difficult to avoid brainwashing, and by and large most of our small group, including myself, were affected by the intense propaganda. Information was thoroughly controlled. China was virtually closed. There was not a single American correspondent in the country and other foreign journalists were permitted to go to only a few select places. Neither Chinese nor China-watchers knew basic facts. Foreigners could not purchase or be in possession of one of the three national papers, *Guang Ming Ribao,* although it was sold in newsstands, hawked on the streets, and seen lying on hotel chairs and taxi driver seats. Statistics in economic reports were falsified. Bookstores were empty except for works by Marx, Engels, Lenin, Stalin and Mao. For ten years the movie theaters played only the eight films approved by Jiang Qing. Unreported were forced migrations for the colonialization and suppression of "minority" culture, particularly that of Uigur and other Turkic and Muslim peoples in Xinjiang, China's largest province. The famine years were 1961–64. In that period apparently more people died of starvation than in any famine in recent centuries. Based on China's own official census reports, demographers suggest that between 30 to 60 million people perished. But famine was undisclosed in China and abroad—although the Red Cross and other international agencies were aware of it; for all intents and purposes it never existed. Starvation in China was another secret gulag. While we were there, no word was ever revealed of fatalities caused by famine any more than by powerful earthquakes in major cities. Word about the 1976 earthquake in Tangshan, the most powerful quake in four centuries, killing over 700,000 people, reached national and international newspapers only in the form of boasting how very advanced Chinese seismologists were in monitoring the movements of domestic animals for predicting natural disasters and preventing human catastrophe. In dispersing and manipulating information, the government maintained a self-congratulatory posture of enthusiasm.

In a strange way, however, these were amazing days to be in China. The very gift of entry, denied to all but a handful, the pioneer view of a country at last partially opened after more than three decades, the experiment of socialism, easy access to "highly responsible citizens," banquets, acupuncture, communes, barefoot doctors, the much-publicized honesty about small money matters—all helped to create a euphoria among the privileged visitors. The common people one met in streets and alleys were obliged to clap whenever we approached. We were called "friends of China" but we didn't know that no one could speak to us privately without risking arrest or, at the very least, unit "criticism." We were aware that homes were off-limits except for a few showplace workers' retirement apartments.

In 1984 I returned to China. The trip had been delayed for a year precisely because I had translated Mao's poems. Later my university colleagues at Beijing Foreign Studies University were to confide in me that they were concerned that I might have been a radical Maoist leftist. Now, by contrast, when people in the new China referred to the Gang of Four they raised five fingers to include Madame Jiang Qing's husband. On my first trip sentences were prefaced doggedly with, "As Chairman Mao says." Now the Great Helmsman, who like Stalin has been declared 70 percent good, was seldom invoked.

All my life I had wished to write a book of poems while in China (*China Poems* was written two years after I left the country), a book as personal and self-reflexive as any I might write elsewhere. So from the first days after my arrival I began this present volume. The year in the mainland affected me personally in very decisive ways, which in turn affected my perspective of the country. I devoted my time so completely to the poems and to a volume of poems by the Tang Buddhist nature poet Wang Wei (701–761), translated with my son Tony Barnstone and student Xu Haixin, that I often worried I would not have time to see what I was trying to write about. But time is distinct and generous in China. What I did see and feel is recorded in *Five A.M. in Beijing*.

*

My editor and publisher, Stanley Moss, asked me to write this brief afterword. I thank him for allowing me to remember early days in China and for reading these poems with care. He rigorously tested me through each poem. In fact he has been the ideal reader, who not only caught bad passages but frequently suggested specific changes that saved and sharpened a poem. I am grateful. I am equally grateful to Tony Barnstone, with whom I shared the year in China, who went over each poem with a relentless 4B pencil, seeking out repetitions, fuzziness and weak lines.

115

Books by Willis Barnstone

Poetry

From This White Island (Twayne, 1959)
A Day in the Country (Harper & Row, 1970)
New Faces of China (Indiana, 1972)
China Poems (Missouri, 1976)
Stickball on 88th Street (special issue of Colorado Quarterly, 1978)
Overheard (Raintree, 1979)
A Snow Salmon Reached the Andes Lake (Curbstone, 1980)
Ten Gospels & a Nightingale (Triangular, 1981)

Criticism

The Poetics of Ecstasy: Varieties of Ekstasis from Sappho to Borges
   (Holmes & Meier, 1983)
The Other Bible: Jewish Pseudepigrapha, Christian Apocrypha, Gnostic Scriptures
   (Harper & Row, 1984)
Borges, Poets of Ecstasy (St. Luke's Press, 1985)
The Double Art: Translation History, Theory & Practice (Yale, forthcoming)

Translations

The Other Alexander by Margarita Liberaki (with Helle Tzalopoulou Barnstone),
   (Farrar, Straus, and Giroux [Noonday], 1959)
Greek Lyric Poetry (Bantam, 1962; Schocken, 1972)
Sappho (Doubleday, 1965)
Physiologus Theobaldi Episcopi (Indiana, 1964)
The Song of Songs (Kedros, Athens, Greece)
The Poems of Saint John of the Cross (New Directions, 1967)
The Unknown Light: The Poems of Fray Luis de Leon (SUNY, 1979)
My Voice Because of You by Pedro Salinas (SUNY, 1976)
The Poems of Mao Tse-tung (Harper & Row, 1972)
The Dream Below the Sun: Selected Poems of Antonio Machado
   (Crossing, 1981)
Bird of Paper: Selected Poems of Vicente Aleixandre (Ohio University, 1981)
Spanish Poetry (University of California, forthcoming)

Anthologies

A Book of Women Poets from Antiquity to Now, ed. with Aliki Barnstone (Schocken, 1980)
Eighteen Texts (Harvard, 1972)
Borges at Eighty: Conversations (Indiana, 1972)

About the Author

Willis Barnstone was born in Lewiston, Maine and educated at Bowdoin, Columbia, and Yale. He spent ten years living and working in Spain, France, and Greece. He has also travelled widely and lived in South America and the Orient. He was Fulbright Professor of American Literature at Beijing Foreign Studies University 1984–85. In addition to volumes of his poetry and criticism, his translations from ancient and modern languages testify to his service to an Himalayan range of cultures and languages.

He has been a Guggenheim Fellow and recipient of NEH and NEA Fellowships. Mr. Barnstone has collaborated with his daughter Aliki and his son Tony on anthologies and translations. He is currently professor of Comparative Literature and Spanish at Indiana University.